PEOPLES of NORTH AMERICA

Hopi

VALERIE BODDEN

CREATIVE EDUCATION · CREATIVE PAPERBACKS

Published by Creative Education and Creative Paperbacks
P.O. Box 227, Mankato, Minnesota 56002
Creative Education and Creative Paperbacks
are imprints of The Creative Company
www.thecreativecompany.us

Design and production by Christine Vanderbeek
Art direction by Rita Marshall
Printed in China

Photographs by Alamy (Aurora Photos, John Cancalosi, CH Collection, ClassicStock, CrackerClips
Stock Media, Tom Daniel, Paul Fearn, Glasshouse Images, George H.H. Huey, Lebrecht Music and
Arts Photo Library, National Geographic Creative, Chuck Place, The Protected Art Archive, Lee
Rentz, Don B. Stevenson, Universal Images Group North America LLC, Jim West, World
History Archive), Creative Commons Wikimedia (George Grantham Bain/Library of Congress,
Billy Hathorn), Dreamstime (Sandra Foyt, Isselee, Nuvista, Linda Williams), Shutterstock
(Dennis W Donohue, Everett Historical, Rick Grainger, A.Hornung, SMIRNOVA IRINA,
KellyNelson, kojihirano, OHishiapply, Transia Design, Arlene Treiber Waller)

Library of Congress Cataloging-in-Publication Data
Names: Bodden, Valerie, author.
Title: Hopi / Valerie Bodden.
Series: Peoples of North America.
Includes bibliographical references and index.
Summary: A history of the people and events that influenced the North American Indian tribe
known as the Hopi, including chief Lololoma and conflicts such as the strip-mining of Black Mesa.
Identifiers: LCCN 2017035416 / ISBN 978-1-60818-965-6 (hardcover) /
ISBN 978-1-62832-592-8 (pbk) / ISBN 978-1-64000-066-7 (eBook)
Subjects: LCSH: Hopi Indians—Social Life and Customs—
Juvenile literature. / Hopi Indians—History—Juvenile literature.
Classification: LCC E99.H7 B59 2018 / DDC 979.1004/97458—dc23

CCSS: RI.5.1, 2, 3, 5, 6, 8, 9; RH.6–8.4, 5, 6, 7, 8, 9

First Edition HC 9 8 7 6 5 4 3 2 1
First Edition PBK 9 8 7 6 5 4 3 2 1

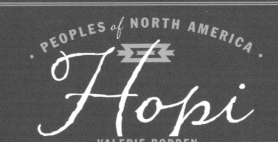

· PEOPLES *of* NORTH AMERICA ·

Hopi

VALERIE BODDEN

CREATIVE EDUCATION · CREATIVE PAPERBACKS

Table of Contents

⟶⊸   A HOPI SNAKE PRIEST PERFORMING THE SNAKE   ⊶⟵
DANCE (ON PAGE 3); A REPLICA OF A PUEBLO IN
GRAND CANYON NATIONAL PARK (PICTURED HERE).

Introduction

More than a thousand years ago, the American Indians known as the Hopi settled along three **MESAS** at the edge of the Painted Desert of the American Southwest. Rising 600 feet (183 m) above the dry land below, the rocky mesas stood like fingers poking out into the desert. Between them, sandy valleys boasted sparse growths of spiny cholla cactus. The scent of sagebrush wafted on desert winds. Scant game roamed this silent land, although rabbits scurried through the brush, and lizards left their tracks in the sand. At the edges of the mesas, springs provided life-giving water in an otherwise dry region. What moisture did fall often came in torrents, temporarily raging down typically dry streambeds. Living in homes that appeared to grow out of the rocky mesas, the Hopi farmed this arid land, making use of every available water source. For the Hopi, the land and water were vital to their way of life.

The name "Hopi" is a shortened version of *Hopituh Shi-nu-mu*, which means "one who follows the path" or "peaceful people" in the Hopi language. Throughout their history, the Hopi have striven to maintain peace and balance in all they do. Yet their peaceful way of life was threatened by newcomers, including Spanish and American settlers. The settlers' arrival led to rifts between traditional Hopi, who wanted to hold on to their ways, and progressive Hopi, who wished to adopt the ways of the settlers. Although tensions remain between the two groups, today's Hopi retain much of their traditional culture, which they pass on to new generations.

THE PAINTED DESERT IS A BADLANDS AREA NAMED FOR THE COLORFUL ROCK LAYERS STRIPING ITS LANDSCAPE.

· HOPI ·

The Oldest People

PEOPLES of NORTH AMERICA

Other American Indian peoples call the Hopi "the oldest of the people." The Hopi belong to the family of Pueblo Indians. They lived farther west than any other Pueblo group. Most other Pueblo peoples lived along the Rio Grande and its tributaries in present-day New Mexico. But the Hopi lived near the Grand Canyon in present-day Arizona.

ANTHROPOLOGISTS believe that the Hopi, like all Pueblo Indians, descended from earlier inhabitants of the Southwest known as the Ancestral Pueblo, or Anasazi. The name *Anasazi* comes from a Navajo Indian word meaning "ancestors of the enemy." The Hopi call their ancestors the *Hisatsinom*, or "Ancient People."

The Anasazi are believed to have entered the Southwest around A.D. 100. They spread through the Four Corners region of the United States. This area is where the states of Colorado, Utah, New Mexico, and Arizona meet. The Anasazi built circular pit houses. These homes were constructed partially underground and had walls made of branches woven together and covered with earth. The Anasazi hunted the region's sparse game and gathered wild seeds and fruit. Later, they began to farm as well. Over time, farming became more important, although some hunting and gathering continued. Elaborate

A GROUP OF ANASAZI NICKNAMED THE "BASKET-MAKERS" LIVED IN PIT HOUSES ATOP MESA VERDE IN PRESENT-DAY COLORADO.

ANASAZI CLIFF DWELLINGS WERE PROTECTED FROM INTRUDERS, THANKS TO LADDERS THAT COULD QUICKLY BE RETRACTED.

baskets were used to collect the food, which was stored in underground pits. These pits were often lined with stone slabs. They were covered with twigs, grass, and mud. This kept the food from spoiling. It also kept animals out.

By A.D. 700, the Anasazi began to build a new type of dwelling, which would come to be known as a pueblo. Pueblos were made of stone held together by a mortar of heavy clay called adobe. The pueblos of extended families were often connected, sharing walls much like a modern apartment building. These homes were built in deep canyons, on mesa tops, or in openings in cliff faces.

The Anasazi population grew and thrived from 1100 to 1300. But by the early 1300s, the Anasazi had begun to move away from their traditional homes. Scholars have been unable to determine what sparked the move. Drought, lack of food, invasions by other tribes, or disease may have made the Anasazi homeland unlivable. Whatever the cause, the Anasazi split into smaller groups and spread throughout present-day Arizona and New Mexico. Some Anasazi moved onto the three mesas of northeastern Arizona that became the Hopi homeland. They may have mingled with peoples already living in the region.

Located east of the Grand Canyon, the three Hopi mesas made up the southern edge of a much larger formation known as Black Mesa. Named in order from east to west, the Hopi mesas became known as First Mesa, Second Mesa, and Third Mesa. Hopi villages were established on and around each mesa. By 1350, the Hopi culture was firmly established on all three mesas. The **DIALECT** of the Hopi language spoken on each mesa differed slightly. Unlike other **PUEBLOAN** languages, the Hopi language belonged to the Uto-Aztecan language family. It was related to the languages of the Ute

Being Hopi

◈━━ **ANCIENT COAL MINERS** ━━◈ *The Hopi found a ready source of fuel in the coal that made up Black Mesa. Using picks up to 12 inches (30.5 cm) long, hammerstones (rounded stones used for pounding), and broken pieces of pottery, the Hopi dug coal from below the mesa's rim. In some places, they created underground mines as well. In all, the Hopi may have mined more than 100,000 tons (90,718 t) of coal. They used it to heat their homes and kivas as well as to fire their pottery.*

and Paiute Indians of Colorado and Utah.

Each mesa was home to several villages. Within the villages, the people were divided into clans. Clans were made up of extended families descended from a common ancestor. Ancestry was traced on the woman's side of a family. Among the 20 or more Hopi clans were the Bear, Snake, Badger, and Antelope clans. Groups of related clans are called phratries. Each phratry and clan had specific duties within the village.

In each village, the people built stone and adobe pueblos one to three stories high. Logs dragged from distant forests supported a flat roof of poles, branches, and leaves plastered with mud. The roofs kept the pueblos dry and retained heat in winter while remaining relatively cool in summer. Even so, summertime temperatures often drove families to the roof to eat and sleep. The walls of the pueblos had no doors or windows. Instead, the structures were entered through a hole in the roof. Some rooms in the pueblos were used only for grinding corn or storing food. The home's main living space contained a fireplace. Bottomless clay jars stacked together formed a chimney. Because wood was scarce in the desert, homes were heated with coal mined from the mesa rims.

⇒═ **SPIRITUAL INITIATION** ═⇐ *A Hopi's religious life began young. Between the ages of 6 and 10, both boys and girls were initiated into the katsina ceremonies. At their initiation, the youngsters learned that the katsinas seen in the dances were not really spirits but were men of their village dressed up to impersonate the spirits. The initiation ceremony involved* **FASTING** *and praying. The children were also struck with a yucca whip by Whipping Katsinas. Afterward, they were allowed to participate in ceremonies.*

Open plazas between groups of pueblos served as spaces for conducting ceremonies. Within the plazas were one or more ceremonial kivas. These were circular or rectangular underground rooms of about 12 to 20 feet (3.7–6.1 m) across. The kivas were entered by climbing through a trap door and down a ladder. Inside, the kiva's most important aspect was the *sipapu*, a small hole dug in the ground. The sipapu symbolized the Hopi belief that their people had emerged from a cave world underground.

Hopi villages had to be located near springs to meet the people's need for water. Fields were also planted near springs when possible. Despite the dry climate, the Hopi relied on farming for their main source of food. The Hopi's most important crop was corn. According to Hopi educator and artist Ramson Lomatewama, "When a person planted corn, they would be raising these corn plants up as their children. We were taught to sing to our corn, sing to our children, talk to our children, to love our children, to care for them. Corn provides us with food. It is the center of life and the essence of life."

The Hopi grew 24 varieties of corn in every color. They had more than 50 ways to prepare the harvested corn, including

TODAY, HOPI
TRADITIONALISTS
LIVING IN ORAIBI
(PICTURED C. 1901)
CONTINUE PRAC-
TICES SUCH AS MAK-
ING PIKI (ABOVE).

baking it into a thin bread called *piki*. Corn could also be soaked in wet ashes and then boiled and washed. It was baked in outdoor ovens, ground to make cornmeal, or shaped into dumplings. Besides corn, the Hopi grew beans, squash, cotton, and tobacco. Women gathered what wild plants were available, including pine nuts, prickly pears, yucca, berries, currants, nuts, and seeds. Men occasionally hunted deer, pronghorn, and rabbit as well. Long journeys to the Grand Canyon brought back needed salt.

Living on their three mesas, the Hopi were relatively isolated. But they established trade relationships with other Pueblo tribes, including the Zuni and Eastern Pueblo, as well as the Havasupai. Hopi cotton was exchanged for seashells, macaw feathers, and turquoise. The Hopi also faced raids from the **NOMADIC** Navajo and Ute.

Despite these raids, the Hopi were confident they would always remain on their land. They believed it had been given to them by their creator, and as such, it was sacred. Through their fields and their religion, they had a deep connection to the land. They believed they were to serve as Earth's caretakers. As a group of Hopi elders wrote, "The Hopi Tusqua [land] is our Love and will always be…. Our land, our religion, and our life are one."

· HOPI ·

The Hopi Way

PEOPLES of NORTH AMERICA

Hopi life was guided by *Hopivotskwani*, or the Hopi Way. This philosophy laid out a way of life that affected every aspect of Hopi society, from government and religion to family, farming, and art. At the center of the Hopi Way was maintaining balance with nature and with people. The Hopi people believed Hopivotskwani came directly from their great spirit, Masau'u. According to a Hopi delegation, "We cannot do otherwise but to follow this plan. There is no other way for us."

Although they shared a culture, language, and worldview, the Hopi people did not see themselves as a unified tribe. Instead, each village functioned independently of the others, with its own leader, rules, and traditions. Only on rare occasions, such as when facing outside threats, did the Hopi act together.

Each village was headed by its own chief, or *kikmongwi*. In most villages, the kikmongwi came from the Bear Clan. He served as the village's spiritual leader. He also set an example for his people in following the Hopi Way. He oversaw the settlement of disputes among village residents and prayed for the growth of the village crops. The kikmongwi chose his successor from among the sons of his sisters and trained him for the position.

Although the decisions of the kikmongwi could be enforced, he generally ruled by **CONSENSUS** after consulting the leaders of the village's clans. He was

MEN PICKED FROM THE SNAKE CLAN, CALLED
SNAKE PRIESTS, PERFORMED THE SNAKE DANCE, A
PRAYER FOR RAIN.

BECAUSE THEY RELIED ON INFREQUENT RAINS TO WATER THEIR CROPS, EARLY HOPI CHOSE FIELD LOCATIONS CAREFULLY.

aided in his leadership duties by a war chief who might threaten to punish those who disobeyed. Usually such threats were unnecessary. Those who failed to obey were shunned by the rest of the village until they changed their ways. In addition to the war chief, two crier chiefs carried news from the kikmongwi to the people. Each had different duties. One of the crier chiefs announced only ceremonial matters, while the other made **SECULAR** announcements.

Villages had their own land and fields. Each field was divided into several large sections, and each section was assigned to one of the village's clans. Generally, the fields were planted at the base of mesas, where sand had been blown against the mesa sides. The resulting sand dunes often trapped moisture. In addition, run-off from storms flowed down the sides of the mesa, watering the dunes. Fields were also planted in dry washes or at the mouths of arroyos, or gullies, that filled when it rained. Other fields were planted near underground springs. To protect crops from sandstorms, the Hopi surrounded their fields with windbreaks constructed of brush.

Planting took place from April to May or June. Using a hard stick, Hopi men dug a one-foot-deep (30.5 cm) hole and dropped 6 to 12 corn seeds in it. Growing the plants close together enabled the stalks to support each other against strong winds. Beans might be planted in rows between the corn. Squash grew at the edges of the field. By October, the corn was ready to be harvested. It was husked and baked on the cob. The dried cobs were then stacked by Hopi women in neat piles in a storage room at the rear of the

➤➣ ◉ **KATSINA DOLLS** ◉ ➤➢ *Hopi men created elaborate dolls to represent various katsinas. To make the dolls, the men carved and whittled the dried roots of cottonwood trees. They covered the carved figure with kaolin, a fine white clay used in making ceramics. Then, using paints made from minerals, soot, and fungi, they painted faces and costumes on the dolls. The completed dolls were given to children during katsina dances. The dolls were not intended as toys but rather were meant to help children study the katsinas.*

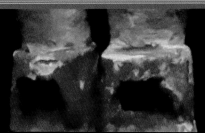

pueblo, to be shelled as needed.

Farming in such a dry land was uncertain. The Hopi relied on their gods to ensure rains. Their religion included many gods and guardian spirits. Masau'u, or the Great Spirit, was believed to have given the Hopi this world and told them how to live. Invisible spirits, called katsinas, were believed to live high on the mountains to the west of the Hopi homeland. According to Lomatewama, "Hopis don't worship katsinas. Katsinas are intermediaries [go-betweens] between the Creator and humankind. They deliver the blessings of life—health and happiness and hope." The Hopi recognized more than 250 different katsinas, many of which took the form of animals, plants, and ancestors.

The Hopi observed numerous religious ceremonies each year. They did this to ensure that the world would remain in balance and the gods would send rain, good crops, health, and peace. Most ceremonies lasted nine days. They involved private prayer, pipe smoking, paintings, and offerings in the kiva, as well as public dances in the plaza. Hopi ceremonies fell into two categories: masked and unmasked.

Masked ceremonies began in January or February, when the Hopi believed the katsinas traveled down from their mountain homes to enter the Hopi villages. For these ceremonies, Hopi men donned elaborate wooden and feathered masks and costumes to impersonate the katsinas. The Hopi believed that when a man performed a ceremony dressed as a katsina, he set aside his own identity and took on that of the katsina. Five major masked ceremonies took place each year, ending in July. After that, the katsinas returned to the mountains. The rest of the year's ceremonies were unmasked. Among them was the biennial Snake Dance, in which participants danced with live snakes in their mouths.

During times when ceremonies weren't being held, religion

THE UNMASKED SNAKE DANCE, PERFORMED BY SNAKE AND ANTELOPE CLAN MEMBERS, REQUIRED MEN TO DANCE IN PAIRS.

AFTER A SUCCESS-
FUL CEREMONY,
WOMEN TRANS-
PORTED RESULT-
ING RAINWATER IN
LARGE POTTERY
JUGS SLUNG OVER
THEIR BACKS WITH
A PIECE OF CLOTH.

still permeated Hopi life. Individuals said special prayers before beginning their daily activities. Men and women shared the work of keeping a Hopi village and household running. Men took care of farming and hunting. Later, after the Spanish introduced sheep, the men watched over the family's flock. In addition, they gathered fuel and spun and wove cotton clothing and blankets. In the mid-1800s, Hopi men took up silverwork, creating highly desired bracelets and belt buckles. The men also served as warriors, although warfare was rare.

Hopi women carried water up from the springs, ground corn, built homes, and cooked. They also made pottery and baskets. Hopi pots were made by coiling long ropes of clay. The clay was then smoothed until no trace of the individual segments remained. Early black-and-white geometric designs later gave way to black-on-orange and black-on-yellow images of birds, animals, flowers, humans, and ceremonial scenes. The women of First Mesa were especially known for their pottery. Second and Third Mesas were

⋙ **WEDDING RITUALS** ⋘ *Hopi men and women generally married around the age of 20. Before a young Hopi couple wed, the bride spent four days living with her mother-in-law, grinding corn and making piki. Meanwhile, the groom and other men in the family wove her wedding belt and two wedding robes. When the robes were ready, the bride wore one for her marriage ceremony. The other she carried in a reed suitcase. When she died, she would be buried in it.*

better known for their baskets, which were made from plants such as yucca and sumac. The plant materials were dyed a variety of colors and woven to create designs featuring katsinas, lightning, and animals.

Hopi women also cared for children. When a Hopi baby was born, he or she was kept out of the sun for 19 days. On the 20th day, a special ceremony was held. The baby received a name and was introduced to the sun. For the first few months of life, Hopi babies spent most of their time in a **CRADLEBOARD**. Young children were also carried in a blanket on their mother's back. As children grew, they were allowed time for play but also began to help with daily tasks. Young boys went to the fields with their fathers. Girls took care of siblings and helped with housework. The Hopi preferred to tease and lecture disobedient children rather than using physical punishment. If children persisted in misbehaving, they might receive a visit from a scare katsina. This katsina had long fangs and bulging eyes and was meant to frighten a child into obedience.

TEENAGE HOPI GIRLS WORE THEIR HAIR IN TWO WHORLED SQUASH BLOSSOMS; AFTER MARRIAGE, WOMEN'S HAIR WAS BRAIDED.

The first Spanish explorers entered what is now Mexico and the southwestern U.S. in the 1520s, claiming the land for Spain. In 1540, Spanish explorer **FRANCISCO VÁSQUEZ DE CORONADO** led an expedition across present-day New Mexico and Arizona. Coronado was searching for the fabled **SEVEN CITIES OF CÍBOLA**. As he rode through small farming villages, Coronado called the inhabitants *Pueblos*, meaning "towns" in Spanish.

Coronado sent one of his men, Lieutenant Pedro de Tovar, along with a small contingent of soldiers and a priest, to the Zuni pueblo of western New Mexico. There, Tovar learned of a group of villages farther west that he believed might be the cities the Spaniards had been seeking. But when he arrived at the Hopi village of Awatovi—the first Hopi village when approached from the east—he discovered no gold. Angered, Tovar and the Spaniards destroyed part of the village and left. Afterward, they visited other Hopi villages, reporting a total Hopi population of more than 3,000. With no gold, Tovar left Hopi country.

For the next 40 years, the Hopi were undisturbed by the Spanish. Then, in 1583, Spanish explorer Antonio de Espejo led an expedition into the Hopi

FRANCISCO VÁSQUEZ DE CORONADO'S EXPEDITION
TRAVELED AS FAR NORTH AS PRESENT-DAY KANSAS
IN ITS SEARCH FOR THE SEVEN CITIES OF CÍBOLA.

TALL KIVA LADDERS
STILL PIERCE THE
SKYLINES OF HOPI
VILLAGES TODAY.

homeland. At first, the people of Awatovi warned Espejo not to enter their village. But when they learned he came in peace, they welcomed him. After leaving Awatovi, the Spanish explorer visited other Hopi villages, where he was also welcomed. When Espejo's expedition failed to find gold, he, too, left the region.

The Hopi were again left alone until 1598. That year, Juan de Oñate led a large group of soldiers, farmers, missionaries, and settlers into the Southwest to colonize the region. Oñate's force waged war against the Acoma Pueblo in New Mexico, executing hundreds. When Oñate demanded the Hopi pledge loyalty to Spain, they submitted without mounting a resistance. But because their mesas were so isolated, their submission did little to change daily life. The Spanish military did not control Hopi lands, and the Hopi paid no taxes or **TRIBUTE** to the Spanish government.

This remained the situation until 1629, when three priests from Spanish-held Mexico arrived in the Hopi homeland. The priests set up churches at the villages of Awatovi, Oraibi, and Shongopovi. Smaller chapels were built in the villages of Walpi and Mishongnovi. The Hopi were often forced to help build the churches. In at least one village, the Hopi kiva was filled with sand, and a church was built on top of it. Most villages resisted the new religion. Sometimes, the people pretended to accept it but continued to worship in their traditional ways.

Although the Hopi did not accept the Spaniards' religion, other aspects of Spanish culture made their way into Hopi life. The Spanish introduced domestic animals such as sheep, which some Hopi began to raise. The Hopi also began growing new crops brought by the Spaniards, including wheat, peaches, apricots, and

⟡⟶ LAYERED PAINTINGS ⟵⟡   *The walls of Hopi kivas were often painted with elaborate murals. These murals might consist of geometric designs or images of animals, birds, or people. The paintings were not intended as decorations but instead were used for specific ceremonies. After the ceremony, the murals were plastered over. New murals were painted on top of them. In some kivas, ARCHAEOLOGISTS have been able to chip away more than 100 layers of paintings and plaster.*

onions, as well as chili peppers from Mexico. European goods
such as iron axes made it easier for the Hopi to cut wood, which
replaced coal as the main source of fuel. Carts drawn by donkeys—
also brought by the Spanish—were used to haul the wood from
distant locations.

Even as they added these elements to their culture, the Hopi
continued to resist Christianity. The Spanish responded harshly.
Items in kivas were burned. In some cases, Hopi caught participat-
ing in traditional ceremonies were whipped in front of the whole
village. Then they were doused in turpentine and set on fire.
Actions like this created hostility between the missionaries and the
Hopi people. Similar conditions existed in other Pueblo villages.

From time to time, various groups of Pueblo Indians tried
to overthrow the Spaniards, but such actions usually ended in
Pueblo deaths. Then, in 1680, all the Pueblo peoples joined together
for the first and only time in their history. The united Pueblo held
the Spanish settlement of Santa Fe under **SIEGE** for a week and laid
waste to the city. On August 10, the priests in every Pueblo village,
including those of the Hopi, were given the option of leaving or
being killed. All five priests living in Hopi villages were killed, and

RUNAWAY STUDENTS *Some Hopi students found conditions in boarding schools so unbearable that they attempted to run away, even though doing so meant facing the harsh conditions of the desert. School officials often tracked down the runaways. Those who were caught faced severe punishments. Hopi Helen Sekaquaptewa reported, "Boys were put in the school jail.... Repeaters had their heads shaved and had to wear a dress to school." Girls might have to "[cut] the grass with scissors while wearing a card that said, 'I ran away.'"*

their churches were destroyed. Ultimately, the Spanish fled New Mexico and Arizona.

In the wake of the rebellion, the Hopi moved all their villages to the mesa tops to more easily defend them. But for the next 12 years, they saw nothing of the Spanish. Then, in 1692, a Spanish force led by Diego de Vargas recaptured New Mexico. Most Hopi villages resented the return of the Spanish. But they pretended to submit to Spanish authority. Because the Hopi were so remote, Spanish officials made no effort to enforce their rule over the Hopi. As soon as the soldiers left their land, the Hopi went back to their traditional worship and way of life. They welcomed refugees from pueblos farther east who refused to live under Spanish rule. Spanish settlers avoided the Hopi homeland; its deserts offered little to tempt them to move there.

Although most Hopi remained hostile toward Spaniards and Christianity, the village of Awatovi allowed the Spanish to reestablish a mission church. By 1700, almost half the population of the village had converted to Christianity. This greatly distressed Awatovi's kikmongwi, Ta'polo. He asked the villages of Oraibi and Walpi to destroy his town. "The women and maidens you take; the

ZIGZAGGED FIGURES OF SNAKES OFTEN APPEARED ON KIVA WALLS, REPRESENT-ING LIGHTNING AND THE ANIMAL'S FUNC-TION AS MESSENGER TO THE RAIN GODS.

men and old women you may kill," he told them.

In an early-morning surprise attack, the men of the other towns burst into Awatovi. Tewaquaptewa, chief of Old Oraibi, described the attack: "The men of [Awatovi] had gone to their kivas…. The men of the [other] villages could look down into these rooms and could shoot arrows into them. They threw bundles of burning wood into them, and tearing down strings of red peppers, they threw them into the fire to torture the men." All of Awatovi's men were killed. Women and children who survived were split up and sent to live in other Hopi villages.

The next year, the Spanish sent a military force to punish the Hopi for what had happened in Awatovi, but the Hopi re-pelled the attack. Further military expeditions in 1707 and 1716 were also unsuccessful. In the 1720s, a few priests attempted to return to Hopi villages but were pushed out. When a prolonged drought devastated Hopi crops in the late 1770s and early 1780s, the Hopi requested food and aid from the Spanish. None was sent. Similarly, an 1818 Hopi request for assistance in repelling Navajo raiders was ignored.

The Hopi noticed little change when Mexico won its inde-pendence from Spain in 1821 and took control of the Southwest. Mexican officials left the remote Hopi lands alone. It seemed the Hopi had successfully preserved the isolation they desired.

Leadership of the Southwest again changed hands in 1848, following U.S. victory in the **MEXICAN–AMERICAN WAR**. Preoccupied with subduing nomadic tribes such as the Apache, Navajo, and Ute, the U.S. government largely ignored the Hopi people. Aside from occasional visits from mountain men or settlers journeying west, the Hopi had almost no contact with whites.

But the Hopi faced increasing attacks by Navajo, Apache, and Mexican raiders. In 1850, a group of seven Hopi leaders traveled to Santa Fe to meet with **INDIAN AGENT** John S. Calhoun and request protection against the Navajo. The next year, the government built Fort Defiance about 100 miles (161 km) east of Hopi lands to establish a military presence against the Navajo. Soldiers from the fort visited the Hopi, bringing with them new diseases. Because the Hopi had never been exposed to these diseases, their immune systems were unable to fight them off. A smallpox epidemic in 1853 was followed by drought and famine. Hundreds died. In the village of Oraibi alone, the population dropped from 800 to 200.

Hopi contact with outsiders increased in the 1870s as Mormon missionaries established churches and even their own city on Hopi lands. The Atlantic and

U.S. SOLDIERS REMAINED AT FORT DEFIANCE UNTIL 1861, WHEN THE ARMY ABANDONED THE FORT TO FIGHT IN THE CIVIL WAR.

AMONG OTHER THINGS, HOPI POTTERY WAS USED TO HAUL WATER, STORE SEEDS, AND COOK AND SERVE FOOD.

Pacific Railroad, completed in 1881, further encroached on Hopi isolation. The railroad brought explorers, traders, and settlers. New towns began to spring up near Hopi lands. Tourists traveled to Hopi villages to purchase Hopi art and pottery. The Hopi also began to trade for manufactured goods from the East.

In addition to increased contact with whites, the Hopi faced renewed conflict with the Navajo. Many settled in regions the Hopi considered part of their homeland. In response to growing tensions between the two groups, the U.S. government established a Hopi reservation in 1882. The reservation included 2.5 million acres (1 million ha) of traditional Hopi lands set aside for the Hopi "and other such Indians as the Secretary of the Interior may see fit to settle thereon." At least 300 Navajo lived on the land encompassed by the Hopi reservation. The wording of the order establishing the reservation allowed more to settle there.

Around this time, several Hopi leaders, including Lololoma, chief of Oraibi, traveled to Washington, D.C. Lololoma was impressed by what he saw there. He wanted the children of his village to have access to an American education. In 1887, a boarding school was established at Keams Canyon, east of Oraibi. Lololoma and his followers eagerly sent their children to the school. But many Hopi resented the appearance of the white school on their lands. A rift developed between those Hopi who accepted the newly introduced white education and culture (who became known as friendlies) and those who resisted white influence (who became known as hostiles).

Parents from the hostile group refused to send their children to school. Government forces responded by riding through villages

❖ **LOUIS TEWANIMA** ❖ *Born in the Hopi village of Shongopovi, Louis Tewanima spent his childhood chasing jackrabbits through the desert. As a teen, he attended the Carlisle School for Indians in Pennsylvania, where he joined the track team. His success there led to a position on the U.S. Olympic team for the 1912 Summer Olympics in Stockholm, Sweden. There he took silver in the 10,000-meter race and set a U.S. record. Afterward, Tewanima returned to Second Mesa, where he tended sheep and continued to run.*

and forcibly removing children from their homes. More than 70 Hopi men who resisted were arrested. Some remained in jail for years.

At the boarding school, children were given new names. Their hair, traditionally worn long, was cut. They were forced to wear American clothing. They were forbidden from speaking the Hopi language or practicing their traditional culture. Those who disobeyed were whipped.

Over the next several years, tensions increased between the hostiles and friendlies, especially in the village of Oraibi. In 1906, the two sides decided they could no longer live together. A line was marked on the stone top of the mesa. Then each side tried to push the other over the line; the winner would remain in Oraibi. The friendlies won the contest, and that same day more than 300 hostiles moved to a location 7 miles (11.3 km) away to establish their own village, Hotevilla.

In the wake of the splintering of Oraibi, the U.S. government established additional schools on the Hopi reservation. In 1934, the government required the Hopi to form a tribal council to act on behalf of all Hopi in matters concerning relations with the federal government. Few Hopi supported the idea of a tribal council, since Hopi villages had always been governed independently. Even after the creation of the council, kikmongwis continued to govern most villages.

In 1966, the tribal council leased Hopi lands to Peabody Western Coal, which began **STRIP-MINING** sections of Black Mesa jointly used by the Hopi and the Navajo. Although the deal brought millions of dollars to the reservation, many Hopi objected to the agreement. They argued that it defiled their sacred lands. In 1971, a group of Hopi leaders sued Peabody Coal and the U.S. interior secretary. The Hopi said that Black Mesa was "part of

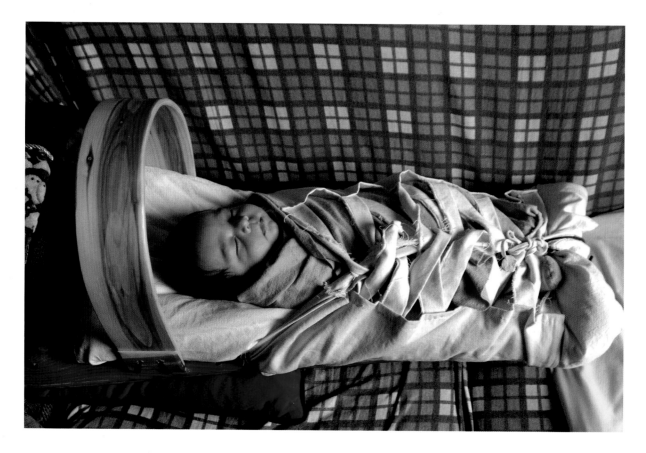

the heart of our Mother Earth" and the strip-mining operation
violated "the most sacred elements of traditional Hopi religion,
culture, and way of life." Although the lawsuit had little effect, the
lease was allowed to expire in 2005.

Another long-standing conflict involved the presence of Navajo
on the Hopi reservation. The Hopi reservation is a small square
of land completely surrounded by the Navajo reservation. Over
the years, the much larger Navajo population had moved onto
parts of the Hopi reservation. By the 1960s, the Navajo had taken
over 1.8 million acres (728,434 ha) of Hopi land. The Navajo-Hopi
Settlement Act of 1974 attempted to solve the issue by returning
about half the land to the Hopi. Thousands of Navajo and dozens
of Hopi living on the wrong side of the new border lines were
given a limited time to move back onto their own tribe's land. The
1996 Navajo-Hopi Land Dispute Act provided the Navajo with
more time to move off Hopi land. By 2018, the Office of Navajo and

⇒ THEY JUST MOVED IN ⇐ *In the 1940s, a Hopi spokesman expressed his people's feelings about their treatment by the American government: "The white men … did not ask if they could live with us. They just moved in. They did not ask what our rules were; instead, they wrote rules for us to follow…. You have put so many of these regulations on us that we are not able to concentrate on the things a Hopi must do, the ceremonies he must keep…. That is why it never rains and why the grasses are scarce."*

Hopi Indian Relocation had assisted more than 3,700 families with expenses associated with the often lengthy process.

Today, the majority of the 14,000 Hopi live in 12 villages on the 3 mesas of the Hopi reservation. Many continue to farm, while others raise sheep or cattle or work in construction or tourism. Disputes remain among those who have adopted some white ways (today referred to as progressives) and those who want to maintain their traditional way of life (referred to as traditionalists).

Despite such conflicts, the Hopi remain closer to their traditional religion and customs than most other American Indian groups. Most Hopi today speak both English and Hopi. Hopi pottery, baskets, and articles of silver continue to be made as well. Hopi villages also continue to carry out many of their traditional ceremonies. As one Hopi chief said, "We … want our way of life to continue on; for ourselves, for our children, and for their children who come after." The Hopi have witnessed many changes in their more than 1,000-year history, from the arrival of Spanish explorers to internal disputes and the establishment of the Hopi reservation. But through them all, they have clung to their traditions and culture, remaining true to the Hopi Way.

HOPI CHILDREN ON THE RESERVATION STRIVE TO ACHIEVE THE BALANCE DESCRIBED BY THE HOPI WAY.

Storytelling was an important aspect of Hopi life. Hopi elders told stories to teach lessons, share information about the world, and entertain. According to one Hopi man, "Everything I have known is through teachings, by word of mouth, either by song or by legends." Many Hopi stories were used to explain and exemplify the importance of the Hopi Way. This story relates the emergence of the Hopi into their land, for which they believed they had a sacred responsibility.

The world we live in now is the Fourth World. The First World was an underground world, in which creatures like insects lived. They were led to a new world, the Second World, where they became animals with fur—dogs, wolves, and bears. Next, they traveled to the Third World, where they became people. They learned to plant corn and make pots. But the world was too cold, and the corn didn't grow.

Hummingbird visited the people and told them of a land above. This land was ruled by the god Masau'u, who controlled fire. From Masau'u, Hummingbird had learned how to make fire. She taught the people. Life in the Third World was good. But the people soon began doing all kinds of evil. A kind spirit named Grandmother Spider told the people they must leave the Third World because it had become corrupted by evil. They had to go to the Upper World of Masau'u.

But the people did not know how to get to that world because it was so high above them. The people asked Eagle and Hawk to fly up to look for an opening into the world above. But neither bird could fly high enough. So the people turned to Swallow. Swallow flew up and up until he found an opening. But Swallow said the people would need wings to get to the hole.

The people didn't know what to do. But then a young boy told the chief about his friend, Chipmunk. Chipmunk gathered the seeds of trees. The people asked Chipmunk to plant a tree that would reach all the way through the sky. Chipmunk planted a spruce tree. He sang songs to make the tree grow faster. But the tree did not grow tall enough. So Chipmunk planted a fir tree. But it, too, was too short. Chipmunk tried another tree, but it did not reach the hole in the sky, either.

Finally, Chipmunk planted a hollow reed. Chipmunk's song made the reed grow until it reached above the clouds. But the people could not climb the outside of the smooth reed. So Chipmunk made a hole in the reed. The people entered the hole and climbed up inside the reed. When they reached the top, they came out in the Fourth World. And that is where they still live today.

ANTHROPOLOGISTS
people who study the physical traits, cultures, and relationships of different peoples

ARCHAEOLOGISTS
people who study human history by examining ancient peoples and their artifacts

CONSENSUS
agreement by all or most of a group

CRADLEBOARD
a board or frame to which an infant could be strapped to be carried on the back

DIALECT
a form of a language that uses specific pronunciations, grammar, or vocabularies that differ from other forms of the language; speakers of different dialects of the same language can usually understand each other

FASTING
going without eating, often as part of a religious ritual

FRANCISCO VÁSQUEZ DE CORONADO
(c. 1510–54) Spanish explorer of the American Southwest who discovered many landmarks, including the Grand Canyon, but not the legendary Seven Cities of Cíbola that he sought

INDIAN AGENT
someone assigned to deal with specific Indian tribes on the government's behalf

MESAS
flat, raised areas of land with steep sides

MEXICAN–AMERICAN WAR
fought from 1846 to 1848 between the U.S. and Mexico over the territory of Texas, the conflict resulted in the U.S. gaining control over the lands of the American Southwest

NOMADIC
moving from place to place rather than living in a permanent home

PUEBLOAN
having to do with the Pueblo Indians, who lived in the American Southwest in large, flat-roofed housing complexes

SECULAR
not related to or connected with religion

SEVEN CITIES OF CÍBOLA
legendary cities supposedly made of gold first reported by Spanish explorer Álvar Núñez Cabeza de Vaca, after he was shipwrecked off the coast of Florida and crossed much of the Southwest, encountering American Indian settlements along the way

SIEGE
a military attack in which an army surrounds the enemy to force a surrender

STRIP-MINING
a mining process that involves removing soil and rock from the ground to reach minerals beneath the surface

TRIBUTE
payment made by one nation to another to show submission or ensure protection

James, Harry C. *The Hopi Indians: Their History and Their Culture.* Caldwell, Idaho: Caxton, 1956.

Josephy, Alvin M. *The Longest Trail: Writings on American Indian History, Culture, and Politics.* New York: Vintage Books, 2015.

Miller, Lee, ed. *From the Heart: Voices of the American Indians.* New York: Knopf, 1995.

Nies, Judith. *Unreal City: Las Vegas, Black Mesa, and the Fate of the West.* New York: Nation Books, 2014.

Ortiz, Alfonso, ed. *Southwest.* Vols. 9–10 of *Handbook of North American Indians.* Ed.

William C. Sturtevant. Washington, D.C.: Smithsonian, 1979.

Page, Jake. *In the Hands of the Great Spirit: The 20,000-Year History of American Indians.* New York: Free Press, 2003.

Sheridan, Thomas E., and Nancy J. Parezo, eds. *Paths of Life: American Indians of the Southwest and Northern Mexico.* Tucson: University of Arizona Press, 1996.

Trimble, Stephen. *The People: Indians of the American Southwest.* Santa Fe: School of American Research, 1993.

⊷≕ READ MORE ≕⊷

Dwyer, Helen, ed. *Peoples of the Southwest, West, and North.* Redding, Conn.: Brown Bear Books, 2009.

Lace, William W. *The Hopi.* San Diego: Lucent Books, 2003.

⊷≕ WEBSITES ≕⊷

HEARD MUSEUM: HOPI KATSINA DOLLS
http://www.heard.org/katsinadolls/index.php
Learn more about katsina dolls and how they are made.

HOPI CULTURAL CENTER
http://www.hopiculturalcenter.com/
The Hopi Cultural Center provides information on the Hopi land and people.